Edition Schott

Walter van Hauwe

The Modern Recorder Player

Volume 1

ED 12150
ISMN 979-0-2201-1382-6

Volume 2
ED 12270
Volume 3
ED 12361

www.schott-music.com

Mainz · London · Berlin · Madrid · New York · Paris · Prague · Tokyo · Toronto
© 1984 SCHOTT MUSIC Ltd, London · Printed in Germany

Photographs by Maarten Brinkgreve
Drawings by Mirjam Boelaars

Contents

To my wife, Tonneke

With special thanks to:

> *Kees Boeke, for his advice,*
> *Shimpei Matsuoka, for the idea,*
> *Mirjam Boelaars, for the drawings,*
> *Maarten Brinkgreve, for the photographs,*
> *all my students, for their problems.*

Introduction

In the nineteenth century a number of musical instruments, such as the violin, the piano and the flute, were given further opportunities to develop their musical and technical qualities, not the least through the intensive and frequent collaboration between soloists and composers.

The recorder lacks a comparable tradition, because it remained silent for about 150 years after its disappearance around the 1750s, until its first revival concert in England at the end of the 19th century. The fact that the player at this concert actually blocked up the thumb hole — assuming that the hole was there by mistake! — illustrates the long way the recorder still had to go before it could at least be taken seriously again.

Later, by the 1950s, the recorder had become widely used in music education, and had become a popular instrument for amateurs, and was also beginning to move towards professional status. In Britain, Holland, Switzerland and Germany the standard of professional performance on the instrument improved steadily, and at the same time important musicological work was carried out by 'early music' players.

In recent times two of the best known soloists, Hans Martin Linde (Switzerland) and Frans Brüggen (Holland), have had a decisive influence on the constantly improving standard of performance. As we have seen, other instruments have been developing continuously over the centuries up to the present time, with the result that avant-garde composers nowadays are writing music that makes almost no concessions to the technical limitations of these instruments. It is interesting that it should be just at this moment in musical history that the recorder should appear on the scene, and restart its development, as if nothing had changed over the last 200 years.

Like Liszt, Chopin, Paganini and other composer-soloists, Hans Martin Linde began to compose his own recorder music, and famous composers such as Berio, Shinohara, Ishii and Andriessen wrote their well-known pieces for Frans Brüggen.

How far the discovery of new techniques, probably not known in the Renaissance and Baroque, will influence the playing and interpreting of early music, is not yet clear, but I am sure that the effect of the new developments will be felt in some way.

Inevitably a few questions arise:

Is the recorder an old instrument in its renaissance, or can we speak of two types of recorders, a traditional and a modern? To what extent is it possible to play old music on a modern instrument, given that we also play modern music on a historical type of recorder? What is more relevant: the feelings and passions of the old composers, the often puritannical interpretation of our musicologists, or our conditioning as twentieth-century musicians? Obviously there can be no doubt about the necessity to discuss these issues, but in the meantime, I would like to suggest that we learn to play the recorder as well as possible, using both the knowledge derived from old literature and our own discoveries.

Basic Technique

We recorder players and teachers all know them: the colleagues with stiff fingers, hands like paws, acute tension in arms and neck, and their invisible lips pressed tightly inwards. That is the way they learned to play the recorder, or to be more accurate, that is the position they arrived at by themselves through lack of proper guidance.

All recorder methods were, and many still are, based on getting instant results: a short explanation about the position of the hands, the thumb-hole half opened, holes 6 and 7 half closed, some air, a tongue, and "hey presto", the first tune can be produced. And that is what parents and grandparents expect, that is what they have paid for; they feel proud that after at the most two lessons, the children can return home with some tangible result. These "systems" usually start with the left hand, typically with the first finger and the thumb (e″ on the treble); they don't go into the question of which hand position will be most helpful to the remaining fingers later on, for instance when playing the c″, or half-opening the thumb hole. And the treatment of the right hand is even worse: starting usually with the a′, (012345) they don't pay any attention to the position of the right thumb. This is rather dangerous, because if the thumb is not in the right place, the lowest note f′ will always be difficult to play, and more or less a lucky accident when it does sound properly.

It is true that children can learn a few well-known tunes in almost no time, and to be fair, why should they know better? After all, the study of the recorder is usually only a form of preparation for the 'real' instrument a year later. We often observe that, if the child wishes to *continue* to study the recorder he either stays with the same teacher and tries to play some more difficult tunes faster, making do with the more or less improvised technique, or (and then he is really unlucky) addresses himself a couple of years later to a professional, and has to change everything, an experience that kills off the enthusiasm of all but the strongest of them.

The aim of this and the following volumes is not in the first place to tell you about the interpretation of old or modern music. Instead, it will concentrate on the less subjective aspects of recorder playing: essentially the technique, and how that technique can be used in a musical way.
While there is already a basic knowledge, evolved over the generations, about how to play the violin, flute, piano, etc., a proper training system for the professional recorder player is missing. I use the word 'professional' deliberately: it is assumed that teaching methods for violin players, even if meant for amateurs, are based on the expertise of professionals, and I see no reason why a recorder method should not be based upon a similar idea.

The art of playing and performing is basically a composite of three kinds of skill:

(a) the purely musical one: the personal "abstract" emotion
(b) the technical one: the purely physical aspect
(c) the so-called "musically-oriented" technique: how to transform a musical idea into the corresponding sound.

A performer, I think, will always try to communicate his very personal thoughts and feelings through his instrument or voice. For this, the first aspect, you need the knowledge of the third, which is impossible to achieve without the second. It is mainly about the second and third aspects of playing that I will write.

These writings are not intended only for pure amateurs: they are strongly addressed to their instructors, for whom it is important to know how to teach the recorder properly, so that children or amateurs who wish to develop their abilities on the instrument more than "just for fun", don't have to start all over again later. And of course this material is intended also for anybody who can find something useful and helpful in it.

Beginning with the purely technical subjects, there are four basic sections:

1. How to hold the recorder — "balanced" playing
2. How to move the fingers — the relaxed "machine"
3. How to breathe — the sound
4. How to articulate — the "speaking"

Why this order?

Before the player can occupy his mind with his final musical story he first has to get all the basic 'equipment' under his belt: he must master all the ingredients as shown in the four parts of this volume:

1. Knowing how to hold the instrument is a basic requirement for free and relaxed playing.
2. The fingers, in fact, have nothing to do with the final sound you produce: they are only the machinery outside the instrument, the "slaves".
3. Breathing is (a) a purely technical matter, the muscles you have to control, (b) a more musical affair, the sort of sound you want to produce
4. The articulation, together with its purely technical aspects and special problems, is the "language" you are speaking: the tongue finally makes your story comprehensible.

If you try to develop the more personal aspects, such as tone and "speaking" first, you will easily get frustrated when your technical ability lags behind your musical progress. If this musical progress makes certain technical demands, it can be very disappointing if these are not met, and this can kill off much of the player's enthusiasm. And there is another reason for this specific order: with a shortage of technical baggage, the student can be too easily influenced by the teacher's solutions and tastes, instead of using and creating his own.

Part I

How to Hold the Recorder

1. The Right Hand
2. The Left Hand
3. The Lips
4. The Fair Distribution of the Weight

General Information

Always keep all parts of your body in their natural position as much as possible.

It will be clear that, when you have to hold an instrument in your hands, and at the same time you have to move your fingers, we cannot really speak about a totally relaxed situation. However it is essential that you know how to strain as little as possible.

When sitting:
☐ sit at the front of your chair
☐ straighten your back
☐ relax your shoulders (keep them low)
☐ keep head and neck relaxed
☐ keep elbows in their normal position (not pressed against or pulled away from your body)
☐ keep your wrists as straight as possible
☐ don't cross your legs
☐ keep your feet in their natural position, flat on the floor

Ill. 1

When standing:
☐ stay in balance, standing straight — do not slant forwards or backwards
☐ keep your back straight
☐ keep your shoulders low
☐ don't let your head hang forward on your shoulders

Ill. 2

Please bear in mind that everyone's hands are different, which means that you and your student should adapt the following explanations according to your own circumstances.

To close the holes of the recorder you need eight fingers, four on each hand; the right thumb takes the weight of the instrument, while the left little finger does nothing.

The numbering of the holes and the corresponding fingers is as follows:

Left hand: thumb is no. 0, and then the fingers are numbered 1, 2, 3

Right hand: 4, 5, 6 and 7 (nos. 6 are also used half-closed, so 6 and 7).

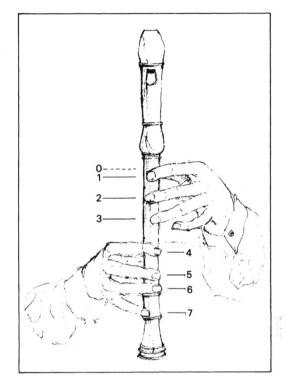

Now we can begin to talk about how to get the most comfortable balance when playing the recorder. Note that all the directions are only suggestions: you will find all kinds of ideas and exercises to develop your own personal way of playing.

1

The Right Hand

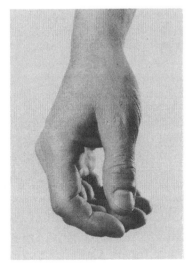

Ill. 3

(a) Hang your right hand beside your body and relax the arm and hand completely. Now look at your hand, and you will see that the fingers and thumb are not straight, but a little bent. (See Ill. 3)

Exercise 1

Stretch fingers and thumb, and relax them again;
repeat this several times:

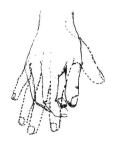

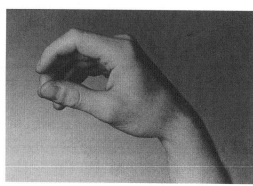

(b) Raise your relaxed hand up and
look through it: you will see a sort
of round "tunnel" (see Ill. 4).

Ill. 4

Exercise 2

Keep your hand in the position as
described in (b), close your eyes
and tap your right thumb gently
and easily with finger no. 4, several
times. Be sure you don't move the
thumb.

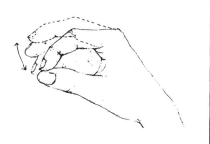

(c) You will notice that, because the thumb and
finger are not opposite each other, you don't
touch the part marked "B" on the drawing, but
that marked "A".

TAKE CARE:

*During the following, keep the natural position of the hand. Don't start by trying to
find the position of the right thumb and then search for the position of the fingers.
Follow the instructions carefully!*

(d) Hold the recorder with your left hand horizontally in front of you, and put
down fingers 4 and 7 on their holes, at an angle of 90 degrees to the
instrument. The right-hand fingers 5 and 6, and thumb, can still move freely.
(See Ill. 5)

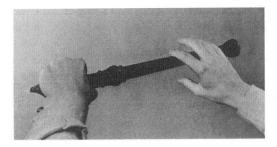
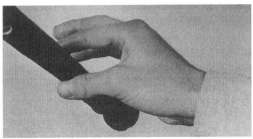

Ill. 5   **Ill. 6**

(e) Close your eyes and move right thumb towards the instrument (see Exercise 2). Be sure that the hand stays in the same position — only move the thumb! It is possible that you may have to make a very small correction here, depending on the shape of your hand. What is important is that you don't touch the recorder with only the tip of the thumb; use half of the top joint — it has to carry the whole instrument!

Exercise 3

● Move the thumb up and down and feel the place where it touches the instrument.

● With the thumb in position, move fingers 4 and 7 up and down alternately, and later in combination with another finger, so for instance, 4 and 7 together, with the thumb in position, then thumb and 2 with 7 in position, and so on.

(f) Now remove your left hand, which means that you hold the instrument only with the right thumb and fingers 4 and 7 (see Ill. 7). Bring the instrument up to the vertical position in front of you (Ill. 8).

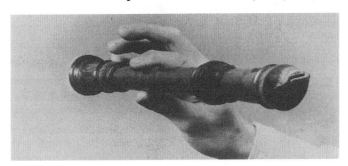

Ill. 7

(g) In this position it's very easy to find exactly the right place for the thumb. You must realise that there is not one position for everybody, but that you should find the position that is most comfortable for you. Try shuffling the thumb up and down a bit, until you find just the right spot.

If the thumb is placed too high, the instrument will fall forwards; if too low, backwards. There is only one ideal place where the recorder can be in perfect balance without straining (see Ill. 8).

Ill. 8

14

(h) When you now put down fingers 5 and 6, you will probably feel that these fingers are just a little too long (if not, don't worry, it can only make things easier). In that case:

Ill. 9a

Ill. 9b

put them down (Ill. 9a)

pull them back a little (Ill. 9b)

push them in, but without straining (Ill. 9c) —everything should be as relaxed as possible!

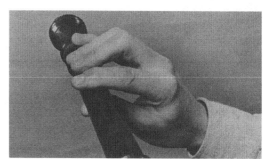

Ill. 9c

Exercise 4

- You have the recorder in front of you, in a vertical position, held only with the five fingers of the right hand.
- Now press as hard as possible on the instrument until all your joints go white with the strain.
- Then relax again very slowly until the recorder almost falls out of your hands (for safety reasons, keep the left hand ready!).
- Just before the instrument is about to fall out of your hands you will achieve the right degree of relaxation of the fingers.

TAKE CARE:

- *Always check the ideal position of the hand: fingers hang above the holes and don't come "from under". Ill. 10 is wrong!*
- *Be sure that the pressing and relaxing is divided equally over all five fingers — don't give all the work to just a couple!*

Ill. 10: wrong!

2

The Left Hand

(a) Follow the same general instructions for the left hand as you did for the right, including Exercise 3

(b) Apply Section 1 (e and g) to the left hand, and you will see that the thumb touches the recorder well under the hole no. 0.

Exercise 5

Move the thumb from its ideal position, in which the recorder is again in perfect balance, to the thumbhole and back, several times.

TAKE CARE:

● *Be sure you move only the thumb and absolutely not the hand or the fingers 1 and 3!*

● *It is essential that you don't close the thumbhole with the tip of the thumb (Ill. 11a) but again with the side of the top joint — half flesh, half nail (Ill. 11b)*

Ill. 11a: wrong! **Ill. 11b: right!**

(c) Finger 2 must find its position in the same way as fingers 5 and 6 found theirs (see 1(h)).

I have often found that players have "problem fingers", fingers that move less easily than the others. Often it is because they started their recorder study with using only one or two "easy" fingers. It prevents a lot of problems later on if the student gets familiar with the use of all the fingers at the same time from the very beginning. The following exercises are intended to encourage this.

Exercise 6

Close all the holes as explained above and move each finger one by one, starting with no. 7 and ending with the thumb.

Exercise 7

Move two or more fingers in all possible combinations, including those "fake" fingerings in the fingering chart. For example: begin with all holes closed, then move 4 and 7 up and down, then 5 and 6, then 4 and 5, 6 and 7, 1 and 7, 3 and 6, 2, 4 and 6; 0, 4 and 6, etc.

16

Exercise 8

Make all kind of combinations as follows: open 4 and 5, close 4 and 5;
open 6 and 7, close 6 and 7; open 1, 3, 6, close 1, 3, 6; open 0, 2, 4, 7,
close 0, 2, 4, 7

Exercise 9

Repeat Exercise 8 in different rhythms, such as:

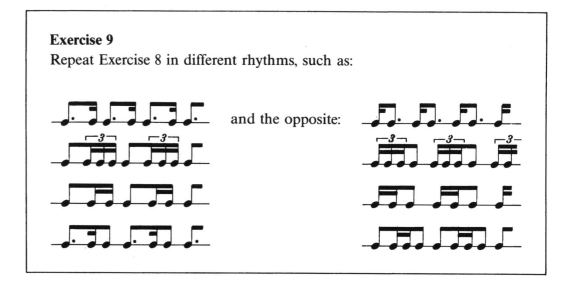

and the opposite:

TAKE CARE:

- *When finding your own combinations, be sure you only move the fingers, and not the whole hand!*
- *Check regularly that the right thumb is relaxed, also the left thumb!*

If, with all these proper hand positions, you put the recorder in your mouth and look along the instrument, it should look more or less as in the first picture (Ill. 12a) and *not* as in the second one (12b).

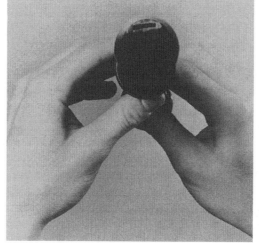
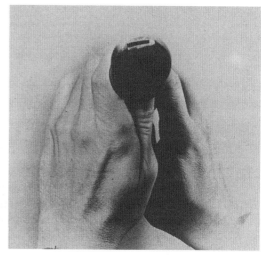

Ill. 12a   **Ill. 12b**

3

The Lips   The mouth, or more strictly speaking, the lips, are very important in this subject.

Because most recorder methods only teach how certain notes are to be played, most students do not realise that they must not carry the weight of the instrument with their left thumb. This problematic finger is in fact the most active one, for it has to do more moving than any of the fingers. If it has to take responsibility for holding the instrument as well, it can easily be strained, by being fixed too much in one place. The following are some hints on how to make use of the lips.

The lips consist of two parts, the weaker part inside the mouth, and the less soft part that we can see when the mouth is closed naturally. The recorder mouthpiece rests just on the border of these two parts of the lip, with the lower lip closing easily around the mouthpiece, using partly the weaker, partly the stronger part of the lip. (See Ill. 13)

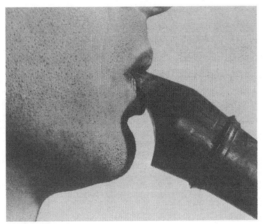
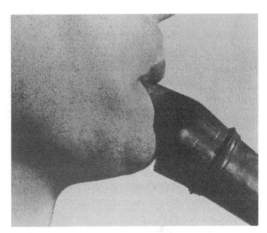

Ill. 13: right!   **Ill. 14: wrong!**

TAKE CARE:

● *Don't keep the upper lip completely relaxed; there must not be a leak between the lips and the mouthpiece.*

● *Keep the lips and jaw as natural as possible, and don't push the lips inwards, or the jaw downwards. (See Ill. 14)*

Exercise 10

Put the mouthpiece far into the mouth and pull it out slowly, with relaxed lips, and you will feel that just when the recorder is about to fall out of your mouth, it lies in the right position as described above.

TAKE CARE:

Bring the recorder to the mouth and lips, and don't bring head and lips to the instrument.

4

The Fair Distribution of the Weight

The weight of the recorder is carried by the right thumb and lower lip so that all eight fingers can be completely free for playing.

Exercise 11

(a) Hold the recorder in the vertical position in front of you as described in section 1(f-g), using only fingers 4 and 7 and the right thumb, with the elbow slightly bent and the instrument in perfect balance.

(b) Slowly, with the hand staying in the same position, move the mouthpiece towards your lips (don't move your head, only, if necessary, the lower arm). Look at the drawing.

(c) More and more you will feel the pressure on the right thumb and against finger 7, while finger 4 has less work to do.

(d) Now lower the mouthpiece slowly on to the lower lip, as I described in the previous section, and you will feel that the lip can increasingly take the weight of the recorder, which will be greatly to the advantage of finger 7 and the right thumb.

(e) The recorder now is carried only by the lower lip and the right thumb, and is balanced by finger 7.

TAKE CARE:

◆ *Don't use finger 4 to keep the balance. This finger loses any carrying function during the course of the exercise — it can even be taken off the hole when the recorder finally rests on the lip.*

◆ *Be absolutely sure that you don't press more than necessary!*

Exercise 12

While holding the recorder as described in Exercise 11(e), bend backwards with the trunk and instrument until the recorder is really horizontal, and be aware of how the fingers and lips feel, especially how free fingers 4 and 7 can be. Bend slowly forwards, until the instrument is really vertical, or even points inwards. You will notice that now you really have to hold the recorder with all three fingers and that you cannot do very much any more with the lips. Be sure that the work is spread evenly over the three fingers.

Of course, both positions are extremes, but therefore at the same time very clear. The usual playing position will be about 45 degrees, which means that, in spite of the fact that lips and thumb have to do most of the work, the fingers 4 and 7 have their duty as well.

Exercise 13
Repeat Exercise 11 and then Exercise 12 now with all the fingers of both hands in position.

Exercise 14
In the position described in Exercise 13, repeat Exercise 8.

A little advice for the more advanced player: if you find in this explanation, or in one of the following subjects, things that you need to change, please change them slowly and with discretion: don't spoil your fun in playing!

Part II

How to move the Fingers

This part will explain something about the actual movement of the fingers when playing the recorder. And I dare promise you that it will be simpler than you might expect.

1. The Movement Itself
2. The Right Hand
3. The Left Hand
4. The "Half-holes"
5. The Left Thumb
6. Which Fingers Do What?
7. Table of Fingerings
8. Exploring Combinations of Fingers

Often, and with both amateur and advanced players, I have faced the problem of a sort of convulsive movement of the fingers, which makes playing very uncomfortable. I think the following explanation can help a lot in solving the problem.

1

The Movement Itself

Speaking purely physically, you can divide the movement of a finger into an upward and a downward one. Let's take the pianists: as well as this upward and downward movement, they have to make a sideways movement: they spread their fingers as well. Even fully keyed instruments such as the flute, clarinet, oboe, etc., sometimes use this sideways movement. We recorder-players only have to move up and down.*

Left hand:	thumb	no. 0 (∅ if half-opened)
	forefinger	no. 1
	middle finger	no. 2
	ring finger	no. 3
Right hand:	forefinger	no. 4
	middle finger	no. 5
	ring finger	no. 6
	little finger	no. 7

Nos. 6 and 7 are often used half opened, so ∅ and 7̸.

Hole no. 8 is the very end of the recorder, and of course you don't have a finger left for it; you need it for some high notes and special tone-colours and it can be closed on your leg. More about this later.

*In connection with shakes, tone-colour and dynamics you will see later that sometimes we have to spread or bend our fingers as well. I will write about this subject later.

For example, a fingering like *01356* means that you have to close these holes with the corresponding fingers.

Exercise 15

(a) Relax your hand — see "How to Hold the Recorder", Section 1(b).

(b) Move only your forefinger upwards, keep it in this position for a few seconds, and feel which particular muscles hold up the finger.

(c) If you now relax these muscles suddenly, the finger will automatically fall back to its starting position.

(d) Repeat this several times and then do the same with all fingers of both hands.

Now, let's suppose that you need muscles for "pulling up" the finger, but you don't need any for "pushing" it down again: the downward movement is relaxing, returning the finger to its place. You can say that it is gravity that brings the finger back.

So, in contrast to the generally accepted idea that one has to *close* the holes, we can conclude that it is actually a question of *opening* them! The starting position is not "all holes open", but *all holes closed* —all fingers down! It is perhaps superfluous to point out that this is a rather important conclusion.

Maybe it is going too far to suggest that the fingers have to do half of the work now, but anyway they have to do less: while you put energy into moving up, the downward movement can fend for itself. My experience has taught me that this suggestion can be a great help, and it always produces results. Use it if it appeals to you as well.

Of course, the fingers have more than only one responsibility, for if they were totally relaxed, the recorder would land on the floor. For these other functions see Section 6 below.

2

The Right Hand

Why start with the right hand?

Experience has shown that the right hand has more relaxation problems than the left, I think because it has to cover four holes with fingers of different lengths, while the left hand only uses three, with the thumb moving in the opposite direction.

Since we first have to be sure of a correct balance, maintained by the right hand and the lips, and the very first note that we play will be the lowest one, it seems logical to begin with the right hand.

Exercise 16
Repeat Exercises 6, 7 and 8.

24

Exercise 17

Study for finger no. 7:

plus finger no. 6:

note the slurs

plus finger no. 5:

plus finger no. 4:

feel the
cooperation bet-
ween 4 and 7

do these exercises slowly as well

NOTE:

☐ Don't use the tongue in these studies, but slur them all: you will hear any imperfections better this way (with the repeated notes try to articulate as "legato" as possible).

☐ All the exercises are notated for the recorder with the so-called "double holes" — I highly recommend this type of recorder!*

☐ Repeat all the exercises as often as necessary.

It's essential that you study these exercises at all kinds of tempi: slow, because your fingers have to learn how to co-operate with each other, fast, because you must learn to play fast as well, to sharpen your ability to react quickly.
Use your own fantasy and creativity to discover other combinations and rhythms: the ones that I have given you are only a few suggestions. Don't make it too easy — it's much more satisfying to work on the difficult ones. If possible, try to practice these exercises together with some colleagues or in a group. You can check and stimulate each other, and it simply is much more fun.

*There are recorders available with alternative, so-called "German" fingering (*01234* instead of *0123467*). On this type of recorder only one fingering is easier, but since I have never encountered any problems with teaching children the *0123467* fingering, I greatly prefer the standard type of recorder. The "German" type has some really bad intonation problems, and will not play all the chromatic notes properly.

3

The Left Hand

Once again I appeal to your own invention and fantasy to think out your own studies for the left hand: it's too easy just to do what you are told, and it will be much more instructive for both teacher and pupil if these exercises are approached in a creative way.

In principle you can do the same exercises as given for the right hand.

Finger no. 0: the thumb can be moved in the same way as I described in Exercise 15. Of course, gravity cannot help here, but the exercises can still be useful, for the thumb needs the same buoyancy as the fingers.

Exercise 18

4

The "Half-holes"

To obtain certain chromatic notes, it is necessary to open some holes partially instead of completely. If the recorder is made properly this applies mainly to holes nos. 6 and 7, so 6 and 7.

This special problem is a big stumbling-block for almost every player and I think many recorder teachers will have had the same experience. The most common fault made is that the player tries to half-close the holes by only bending the 6th and 7th finger, which greatly reduces the speed and suppleness of the whole finger movement.

The technique that I highly recommend is based on turning the whole hand so that the fingers stay in the same position under all circumstances.

NOTE:
You shouldn't think of half-*closing* the particular hole more or less, but remember that you have to *open* it as far as necessary.

Exercise 19

Ill. 15

● Turn the wrist as if turning a door handle, or the volume knob on your amplifier, or as if looking at your wrist-watch. This means that, as a matter of fact, you don't turn your hand, but your wrist!

● Now, take the recorder, finger 0123456 (low g′) and turn your right wrist slowly. You will notice that gradually your 6th finger slips from its hole, until it is completely off the hole, but still touching the instrument.

● Slowly turn it back.

TAKE CARE:

◆ *Don't pull up your finger — it must stay in contact with the instrument!*

◆ *Don't tense the fingers while turning/sliding back.*

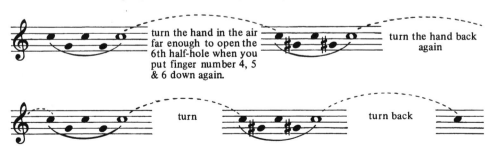

Repeat these motions to and fro, first slowly, then faster, and in different rhythms as well.

You will notice that finger no. 5 is extended a little, but it soon goes back to its place. Finger no. 4 (and possibly no. 5 as well) can be seen, together with the right thumb, as an axle; you will feel hole no. 4 turning under its finger.

TAKE CARE:

Be absolutely sure that you don't move the fingers: always keep them as relaxed as possible.

Exercise 20:

Please repeat Exercise 19 for finger no. 7 (01234567—01234567), and you will see that the principle is the same, only the movements can be smaller.

There are many advantages to this method:
- ☐ The fingers can still move freely when playing.
- ☐ They will not interfere with other movements.
- ☐ It's very safe and precise.
- ☐ It's essential for correcting out-of-tune notes rapidly.

Again, I recommend that you use a recorder with double 6th and 7th holes.

Exercise 21:

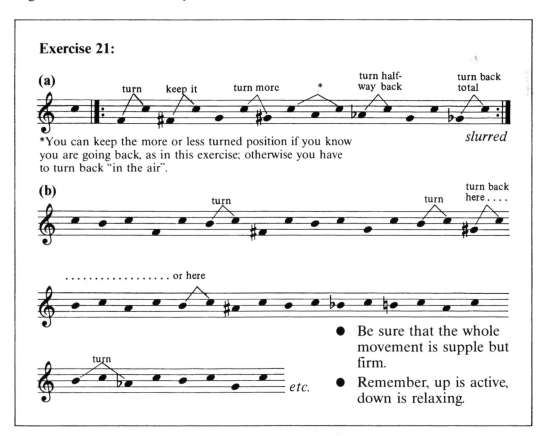

*You can keep the more or less turned position if you know you are going back, as in this exercise; otherwise you have to turn back "in the air".

- Be sure that the whole movement is supple but firm.
- Remember, up is active, down is relaxing.

28

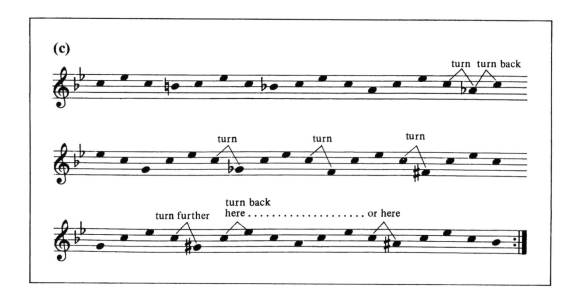

Exercise 22:

To get the c″ sharp in tune on most instruments you have to use the fingering *012456*

etc. as far up as you dare.

And again, find your own variations: it makes much sense to compose them yourself, and it is more more fun.

5

The Left Thumb While the fully-keyed instruments have a special key for it, we just use a special hole, No. 0, which helps us to play the octaves.

There are two systems in use for half-opening the thumb:

(a) drawing away the thumb

(b) bending the top joint of the thumb

In spite of the bigger movement, I prefer the second one, because with this method you can feel the edge of the hole much better, which helps a lot to control the higher notes. And if you keep the thumb on the instrument all the time, there will always be the risk that this already too busy thumb will get involved with taking the weight of the instrument, leading to unnecessary strain.

The principle is that you only move the first joint of the thumb, and not the whole hand or arm (a common fault).

Exercise 23

● Play *0123* (c″)

● Open hole no. 0 by pulling the thumb down

● Bend the top joint (if the second joint moves a little, don't worry, just think of the top joint)

● Replace finger no. 0: hole no. 0 will be half opened now. Be sure that you touch the rim of the hole with half nail, half skin

● Give a little more air and the result will be the high c‴ (*Ø123*).

● Pull down finger no. 0 again, extend it and close the hole

● Repeat this as many times as necessary on different notes.

TAKE CARE:

♦ *Be sure you always move just the thumb and its top joint.*

♦ *Pare your thumb-nail if it's too long, otherwise the air will leak from under the nail, which will produce problems for the higher notes.*

♦ *Don't pinch! The thumb must be just as relaxed as the other seven fingers.*

Ill. 16

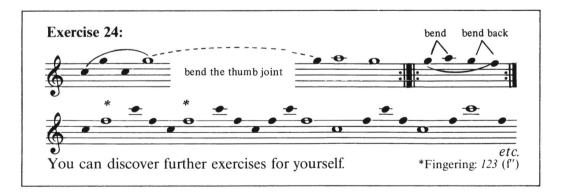

You can discover further exercises for yourself.   *Fingering: *123* (f′)

6

Which Fingers Do What?

I pointed out earlier that the recorder would fall out of your hands if you kept your fingers totally relaxed. Apart from moving in order to produce the various notes, the fingers retain some responsibility for holding the instrument. But remember that the fingers which are moving at a given time should not also be burdened with the responsibility of holding: they must move as freely as possible. It is the others — the ones that are not moving at the time — that are on supporting duty.

Such problems are not very great when you don't have to move too many fingers at once, as in the following example:

All the fingers can help the right thumb and the lower lip a little, except for the 5th finger, which has to move.

It is more complicated with combinations like this:

You will see that to play g″ you need finger no. 2, as well as the thumb and the lip, to keep the recorder in balance: relaxing finger no. 2 completely will result in a very unstable instrument in your hands.

Play and note that in jumping from the g″ to the e″ flat, the responsibility for balance is taken over from finger no. 2 by four others. Be sure that you spread this responsibility fairly! Jumping back means work again for finger no. 2.

I wrote earlier that a falling finger relaxes; that's true, but there is more, for as soon as the falling finger has covered the hole, it has to help to keep the instrument in balance. And there is more still: as soon as the finger touches the hole, the wood should, as it were, "push" the rising finger from its hole, as if the falling finger were pushing the air through the hole under the rising finger.

When playing finger no. 1 "pushes" finger no. 2 off its hole, and back again. If done properly, there will not be a change or any gap or sound audible between the two notes. Check the following:

TAKE CARE:

It's dangerous to solve these problems partly by giving finger no. 0 any supporting work. As I wrote before: this finger must be as free as the others, even more so, because it has to make the biggest movements! So, never, never use the thumb to carry the weight of the instrument. Check this by playing the following:

I recommend that you search for your own combinations. If you teach yourself to be aware of this problem, finally you will notice that you don't have to think about it any more, although, especially in faster movements, it can always be a big help to think of this subject during playing.

7

Table of Fingerings

This list contains the fingerings which are in principle usable on all recorders based on the "baroque" fingering. It is perhaps superfluous to mention that if any interval fingered as described below does not sound right, you should correct this fingering. In this case certain exercises may need to be changed. With all the fingerings shown here, the first one is always the standard one; the others, the alternatives, will be explained later.

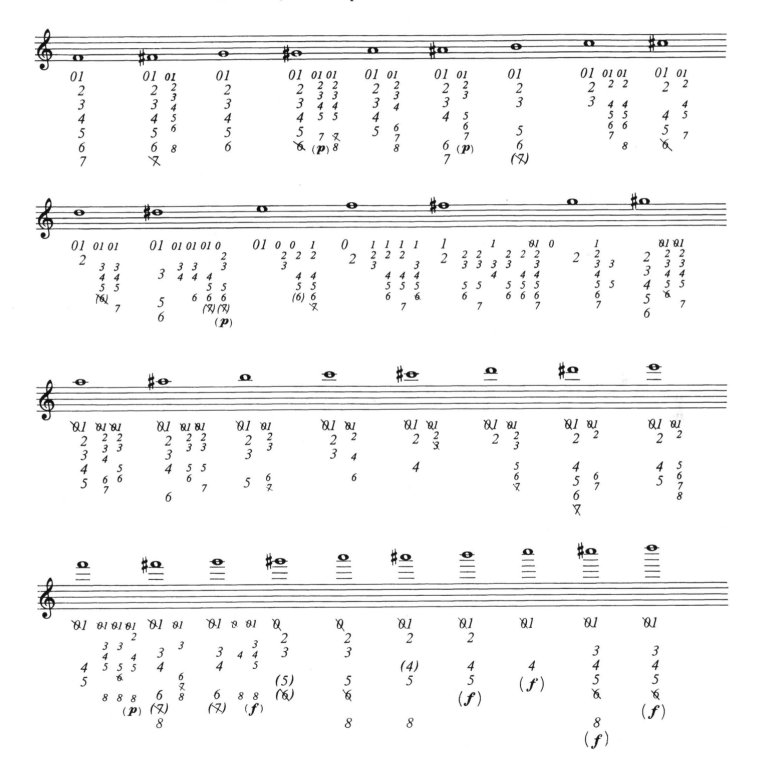

8

Exploring Combinations of Fingers

With this list you can find and compose practical exercises, adapted to your own personal needs.

(a) Exercises with "one-finger" combinations:
(b) Exercises with two moving fingers, or with six:
(c) Exercises with the number of moving fingers increasing or decreasing:

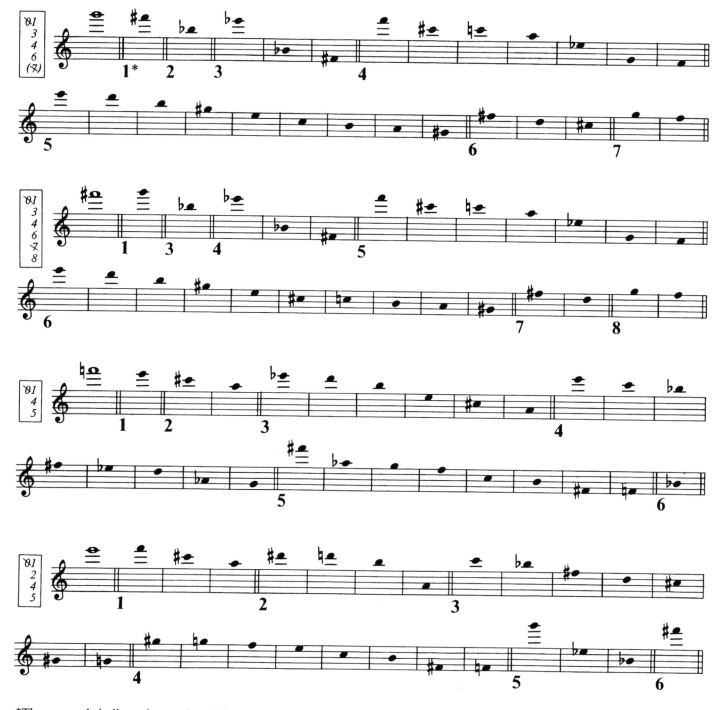

*The numerals indicate the number of fingers that have to move

33

34

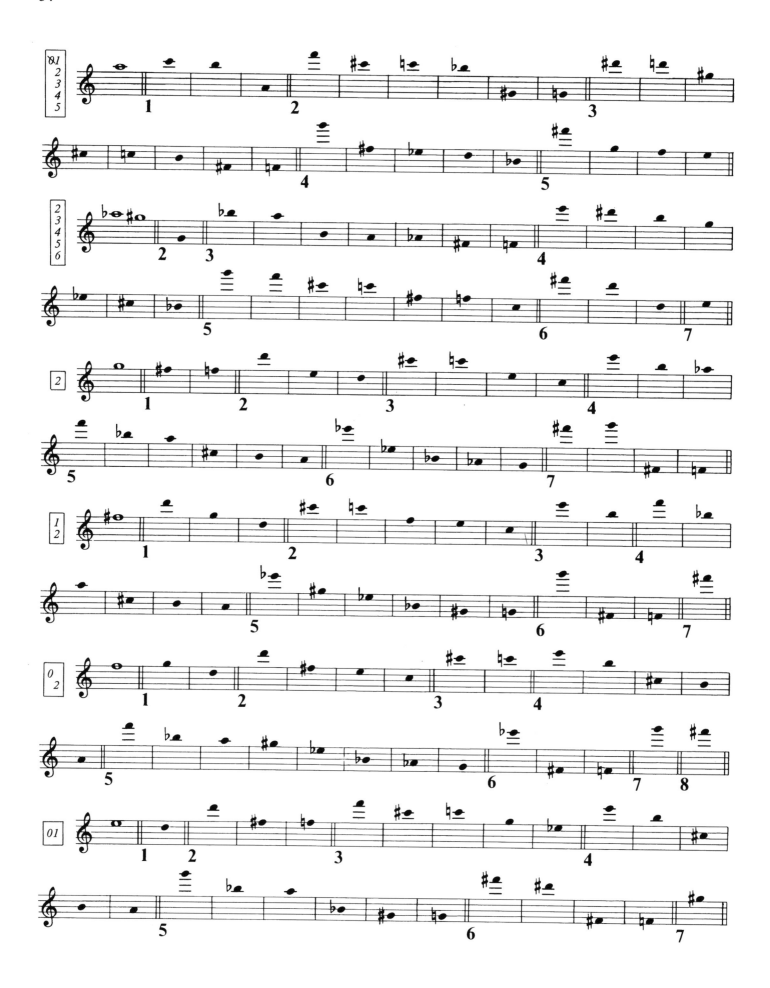

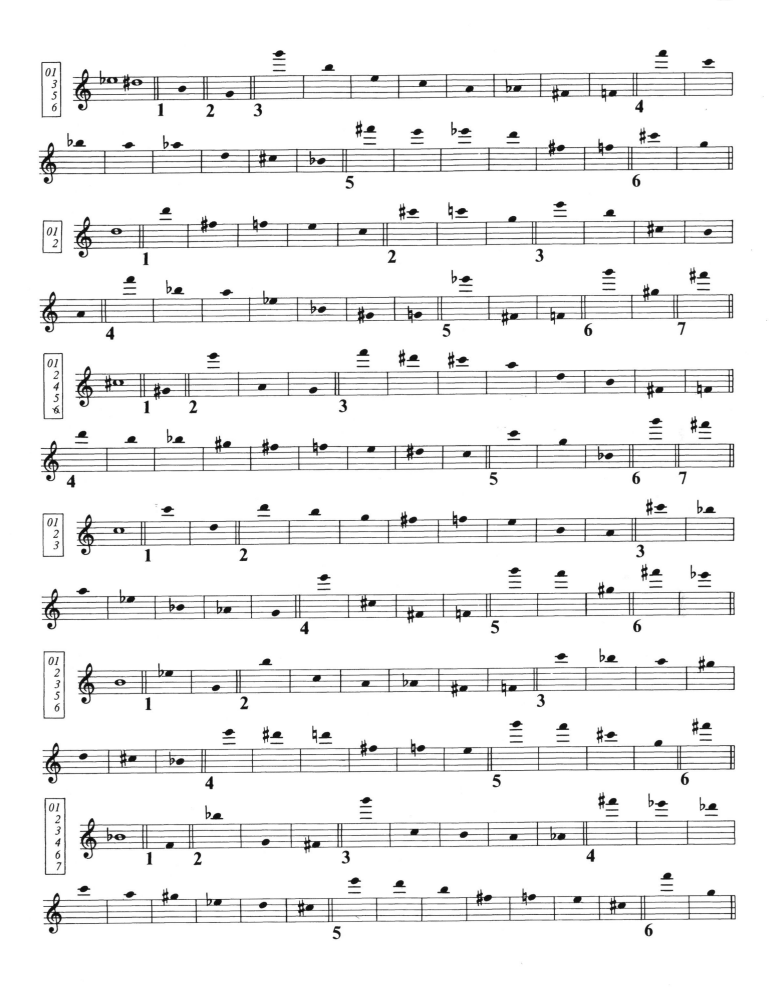

This list gives only the combinations of the standard fingerings. You can work out the combinations of alternative fingerings by yourself.

Part III

About Breathing

If you compare the reaction that Stravinsky's music received in his young days with the great respect it is accorded nowadays, you can get some idea of how quickly people's taste can change: after 35 years Stravinsky and Schoenberg were fully recognised, and in 10 to 20 years the music of Elvis Presley and the Beatles became part of popular culture.

Something comparable must have happened during the second half of the 18th century. Of course there are always certain features of a particular age that cannot be transferred to another, but it is striking that in the 18th century a totally new set of musical values developed. The opera became much more popular, and symphony orchestras became much larger, concert halls began to replace intimate rooms, and so the instruments had to become "real" instruments in the modern sense — louder, bigger, with a wider range, more volume, and the really effective dynamics that were required by the new music. But because most of the instruments were not built to serve such ideals, they needed to be adapted. Thus the clavichord became the piano-forte, the chalumeau turned into the clarinet, and the flute, violin and oboe all had to be changed.

A few couldn't make it. Because of the way they were constructed, they could not be developed: the harpsichord, with its dynamic limitations and comparatively low volume; the lute, with its quiet tone and complicated arrangement of strings; the viola da gamba, which had the same problems (only the double bass, still used in the modern orchestra, could survive); and the recorder, which was soft, too limited in range, with its tuning problems in remote keys, and in particular its inflexible tone quality — the latter possibly the main reason why the traverso was preferred. All the fine crescendos and diminuendos, loud low notes or soft high ones, were not possible on our "simple" instrument, and it was out of tune as well, they argued; I think they were right.

When the recorder was unearthed around 1900, the new players faced the same problems, as the instrument still could not compete with the current "symphonic" instruments. But since chamber music in more recent years has begun to be taken more seriously, the recorder no longer needs to be compared directly with "conventional" instruments. Nowadays players have improved and developed all kinds of old and new techniques which have opened up a whole spectrum of unexpected possibilities.

After talking about the fingers — the machinery, the "slaves" — this part will discuss the basic sound production, the breathing. It shouldn't really be necessary to say that to achieve a rich, colourful and personal sound a proper and effective breathing system is indispensable.

Some ideas and principles found in this part will also be found in books about singing and yoga. Naturally these similarities are not coincidental.

It is possible that for some of you certain statements are expressed too strictly, and some exercises are too extreme. Please learn to select the exercises and ideas which suit your physical and psychological make-up. You may take it for granted that a rigorous and systematic training of the respiratory muscles will provide the comfort and ease to produce a better sound and a finer articulation.

The breathing process can be divided into three main sections:
1. Inhalation
2. Exhalation
3. How to hold the air

1

Inhalation Speaking simply, we can distinguish two types of inhalation:

(a) The high one, mainly done by expanding the chest and by filling the chest cavity. With this type of breathing it is the top part of the lungs that gets filled. It is easy to recognise this kind of breathing: often the shoulders and head rise, and one becomes a few centimeters taller. Watch athletes after a performance.

(b) The low one, which is done with the diaphragm and/or the stomach muscles, and makes space for the lower and larger parts of the lungs.

Although it is possible to combine these two types of breathing, and many players use both, for serious players I highly recommend the second as the basis of the technique, because:

☐ it offers more volume

☐ it is easier to control

☐ it keeps the throat more relaxed

☐ it provides a strong and reliable support for the air-column.

Almost all wind instruments are based on the principle that one has to blow or press the air through a narrow channel with a certain amount of resistance: a reed (oboe, clarinet, etc.), the edge of a hole (flute) or simply an extreme narrowing of the windway (trumpet). The respiratory muscles can easily press the air up to this point of resistance; it's here that the required quantity of air is regulated. But the recorder works quite differently. Whatever the limitations of the instrument, there is one very positive thing that has to be admitted — the perfection of the windway principle. The air column can travel unimpeded to the point where the air is divided. There is no way of influencing the direction of the air column or the quality of the sound by pressing the lips more or less. With the recorder one cannot speak of an embouchure, because there simply is none.

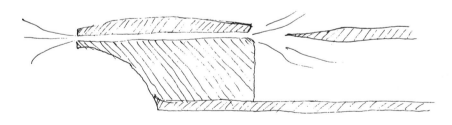

As you can see in the drawing, part of the airstream disappears immediately when it hits the edge, while the other is sent through the entire instrument. To get the purest sound that the recorder has to offer, it is essential that one pays attention to the right proportion between the outgoing and the ingoing air. But since the maker of the instrument has to fix the windway, the player can influence this proportion only with the air pressure. Too much or too little pressure will, generally speaking, always have a negative effect on the tone quality.*

*Later we will talk about the small margins that one does have, and can use.

For a free and open tone, nothing should interrupt the airstream between the air reservoir (lungs) and the lip, where the air is divided. That means that only the right amount of air that is needed for a given sound should leave the lungs. Naturally this requires a strong and controlled use of the respiratory muscles. The following instructions will give you exercises to strengthen these muscles.

About the Diaphragm

I will not go into too much detail about this, but will restrict myself to its function in playing.

The diaphragm is a unique group of muscles, that separates the heart and lungs from the bowels. It is a tendon plate shaped like a clover leaf, situated just below the heart, surrounded by flat bundles of muscles that connect it with the inside wall of the chest, the first lumbar vertebra, the lower ribs and the the lower part of the chest bone. When the muscles are contracted, the diaphragm is flattened, giving the heart and more particularly the lungs more space, and the abdomen is contracted also. You can feel your diaphragm from the back (just above the tailbone) and follow it round, via the floating ribs, to the underside of the chest bone. (NB that with women the respiratory muscles are situated slightly higher than with men). I think that the following exercises will help to locate the diaphragm.

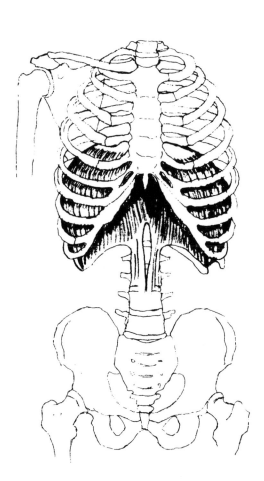

Exercise 25

(a) Take a flower and sniff it, breathing in as deeply as possible (don't use your shoulders)

        or

(b) Pant like a little dog

        or

continues opposite

(c) Lie on the floor on your back, relax, and concentrate on your breathing; you will notice that if you want to breathe high, you have to move your shoulders over the floor, which doesn't feel very comfortable, so instead of that, in- and exhale with the diaphragm and abdominal muscles, something that will happen almost automatically.

or

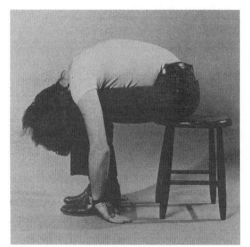 

Ill. 17   **Ill. 18**

(d)

● Sit on the front of a chair, feet flat on the floor, and bend over until your chest rests on your knees and your hands hang on the floor. Without forcing you will automaticaly feel the movement of your diaphragm (see Ill. 17).

● Put your hands on your hips
  - inhale slowly, but as deeply as possible
  - hold your breath for a few seconds
  - exhale slowly
  - repeat this several times (Ill. 18).

● Now, while breathing in and out steadily, with your hands still on your hips, slowly rise, until you are sitting straight again: continue breathing in and out all the time, taking about three seconds per cycle — the complete rising movement should take at least 25 seconds.

Because you can feel the diaphragm much better when you bend over than when sitting straight, repeat this exercise as often as necessary, until you don't have any difficulty at all in feeling your diaphragm while sitting straight or standing.

TAKE CARE:

When you breathe out, you never squeeze out all the air from your lungs: there will always be some left. While the inhalation can be more or less overdone, thus taking in more air than is actually necessary, the exhalation must just follow nature — don't press your brains out! Later on, when we apply the breathing exercises to actual playing, the exhalation will also be more controlled.

Notice that when the diaphragm is completely extended, you will see from the outside a more or less "hollow" stomach. (See Ill. 19).

Ill. 19

A lot of extra space can be created by expanding the abdominal muscles. Now the lower, wider parts of the lungs get much more opportunity to fill themselves to their full capacity. The abdominal muscles are much easier to control:

☐ Inhale, while making a "fatty", a fat stomach —find the band of your trousers.

☐ With the air that is still left, blow as strongly as possible on your hand (see Ill. 20).

☐ Then pull away your hand suddenly, and you will immediately feel an abrupt tightening of the abdominal muscles (Ill. 21).

☐ Repeat this until you can locate and move these muscles independently.

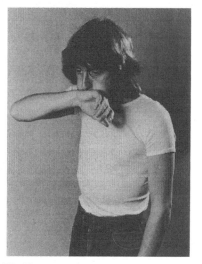

Ill. 20

Ill. 21

If you still can't find these muscles, the following may help. Incidentally, the abdominal muscles are the same group of muscles (usually functioning together with the diaphragm) as those one uses to defecate.

For the sake of convenience, let us call the diaphragm the *side* breathing and the abdominal muscles the *front* breathing.

Exercise 26

- Sit at the front of your chair, feet flat on the floor, and straighten your back (of course, you can stand up as well).

- Put you elbows out and your hands on your floating ribs, and move the thumbs round to feel your diaphragm on your back (remember the remark above about the differences between men and women in this respect), and the four fingers forward to feel the diaphragm on the front, and then the abdominal muscles.

- Inhale, in eight little gusts (jerking), four a second, starting with the lungs empty and filling them up completely.

III . 22

TAKE CARE:

Be sure that all the little gusts are equal, and done only with the diaphragm (after paying attention to the previous suggestions in Exercise 25(d) and studying the photos, you must be able to locate your diaphragm by now — if not it won't make any sense to continue the exercises).

I recommend that you begin the inhalation exercises through the nose, later changing to the mouth.

In the tempo that you are counting, turn your head continuously left and right and back, to keep the throat free and the muscles of the shoulders and neck quite relaxed. (Look at the drawing).

- Exhale, again in eight jerky gusts
- Repeat this as often as necessary.

44

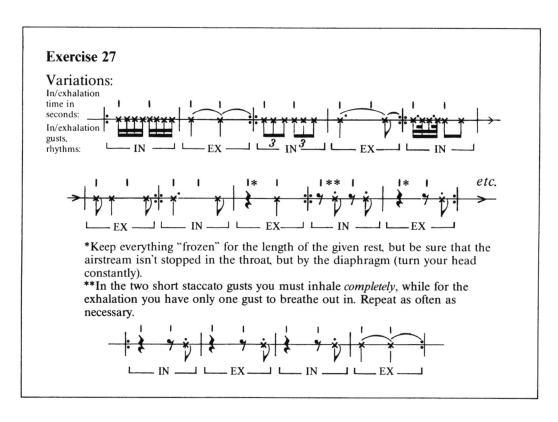

Exercise 27

Variations:

In/exhalation time in seconds:

In/exhalation gusts, rhythms:

*Keep everything "frozen" for the length of the given rest, but be sure that the airstream isn't stopped in the throat, but by the diaphragm (turn your head constantly).
**In the two short staccato gusts you must inhale *completely*, while for the exhalation you have only one gust to breathe out in. Repeat as often as necessary.

Note that in each bar every in- or exhalation has to result in a complete refilling or emptying of the lungs.
Of course you can invent your own rhythms and variations for this exercise.

Exercise 28

Repeat Exercise 27, but now use only the abdominal muscles. It's essential that you take Exercise 28 as seriously as you took Exercise 27.

Exercise 29

A group exercise:

- bar 1: inhale on "sha"
- bar 2: exhale on "tsu"
- bar 3: inhale on "ffu"
- bar 4: exhale on "chi" (as in "chilly")

If done well you will hear four sorts of hissing sounds. Practise this exercise with both the side and the front breathing. This again is just an example — try to find your own different exercises.

Now we are going to combine both breathing systems.

First in slow motion:
1. inhale, using only the diaphragm, (see Ill. 23) then
2. inhale with the front breathing (Ill. 24)
3. exhale, only with the front breathing (Ill. 25)
4. exhale with the side breathing (Ill. 26).

Ill. 23

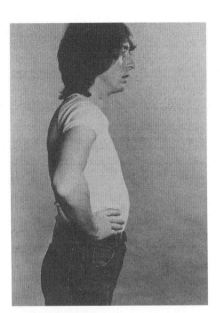

Ill. 24

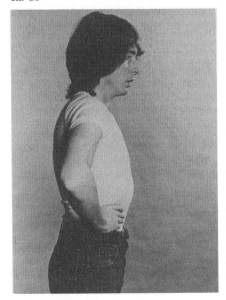

Ill. 25

Ill. 26

NOTE:

☐ When playing you will generally use only the front breathing; the side breathing, i. e. the diaphragm, stays out all the time until the end of the piece, to support the front breathing, and to keep some air in reserve.

☐ Later you will see that the inhalation will be done with both side and front at the same moment; the exhalation on the contrary, will be, in principle, always divided into these two movements.

Exercise 30

Inhalation Exercise:

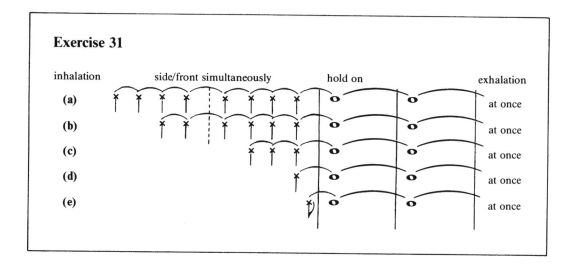

*first through the nose, later through the mouth, but remember the suggestion about turning the head from left to right, in order to keep the air channel totally free and open.

**see Exercise 26, 27 and also 29

TAKE CARE:

● *Be sure the inhalation fills the lungs completely, irrespective of the number of notes you spread it over:*

● *Keep the throat open!*

You will notice that in Exercise 30(e) it becomes difficult to tell apart the side and front breathing. However, I do recommend you to take this exercise seriously, before proceeding to the simultaneous inhalation.

Exercise 31

It is a good idea, before each exercise, to breathe a few times normally, in order to relax the respiratory muscles and those of the neck and shoulders.

2

Exhalation   When breathing in the muscles used change from a state of relaxation to one of tension, and remain that way. By contrast breathing out is a constant, contrary activity, in which the muscles must not sag, for they are responsible for a continuous pressure, and have to counteract the diaphragm that stays flat, i.e. in the inhaling position. In fact we have reversed the natural association: inhale/ activity—exhale/passivity, and this brings us to the conclusion that totally relaxed breathing is a bit of a myth! (remember that our subject is not the kind of breathing used to relax body and mind, but to find a breathing system that guarantees us a flexible sound production).

With a proper breathing system for the recorder one cannot speak about a nice and relaxed feeling, but, after good and serious training, the player will get used to the somewhat tensed feeling in the muscles. It's just as in athletics: training makes the muscles stronger, but also more supple. And, to pursue the analogy, it's important to be patient: regular training does more good than impatient hectic practice.

Exercise 32

(a) Breathe in (side and front) in two seconds

(b) Fix the muscles

(c) Begin to breathe out, but as little as possible, on *ssssse* (air leaking over the tip of the tongue) for five seconds — use the vowels *e* and *i* (from "is") after the *ssss*, rather than *o* or *u*, which can push the jaw down too much.

(d) Interrupt the airstream by simply pushing up the tip of the tongue against the palate. If you take the word "Stitch", pronouncing a long drawn-out *SSSSStitch*, you will get the right effect interrupting the *SSSS*, as you start with the first *T*. You will only move the very tip of the tongue; you should then 'freeze' for, say, another five seconds.

(e) Release the tip of the tongue and breathe out again (the *SSSS* continues automatically) for another five seconds. As little air as possible should escape now. Use only the front breathing — the side breathing will last all the time.

(f) Repeat (d) and (e) again and again, until the front breathing is totally exhausted, and you find yourself with a "hollow" stomach and a still strongly expanded diaphragm (just like a little boy pretending to be a "body-builder") — not a very comfortable feeling.

(g) Continue to breathe out the air, held and supported by the diaphragm, until the lungs are completely empty. It is possible, after rigorous and systematic training, to achieve a duration of about 40 seconds; for the extra capacity that makes playing so much more comfortable I strongly recommend trying to achieve an even longer breath: it is possible to sustain it for up to a minute and a half.

TAKE CARE:

● *If you are not used to the slow release of the air, your body may protest by making you feel dizzy. If this happens, just stop for a moment; you will soon get used to it.*

● *Don't forget to turn your head from side to side during this exercise. Shoulders and neck must be relaxed, as well as the throat.*

3

How to Hold the Air

This subject is perhaps the most important part of the process, and will help to understand the previous section.

When we consider the unimpeded journey that the airstream makes from the lungs up to the lip of the recorder, together with the small quantity of air needed to produce a sound on the instrument, inevitably the question arises whether we can still speak of really blowing. In fact what we are talking about is only regulation of the air, in quantities similar to those used in normal breathing.

Often we hear the recorder played in a loud and gasping manner. While players of this type always think that they do not have enough air, the reality is that:

- they are always taking in too much air

- they don't have the proper technique to store and keep the air in the lungs, which means that more air than necessary flows up towards the instrument, where it will be regulated by shutting or tightening the throat, and/or will be allowed to leak through the nose.

In particular, this exhalation through the nose during playing seems to be rather common. The drawbacks are clear:

- the pressure required for a steady sound falls off

- the passage through the nose is so wide and comfortable, that a player will run out of air in a couple of bars. Typically he breathes rather heavily (because of the quantity of air taken in), but uses only a small proportion of the air to produce a sound. What a waste of energy!

The idea is that you keep the air, with the help of your respiratory muscles, in your lungs, even with a completely open throat and mouth. Your tongue (articulation will be explained in the next part) with its precise "explosions", soft or hard, will have the first responsibility for the way the tone arises. This means: a higher tone needs more "gunpowder" in the tip of the tongue, a lower one less — in short, don't change the air pressure, but adapt the articulation.

Exercise 33

(a) Breathe in as described

(b) Hold: as soon as the lungs are completely filled, you "freeze" all respiratory muscles involved (be sure that the shoulders, neck, head, throat, etc., are not involved — turn your head from side to side again).

(c) Next, open your mouth rather wide (not ridiculously so) and place your hand very close to it, so that you almost touch your nose. If you are doing this properly you should not feel any air on your hand, so that if you use a mirror instead of your hand, no condensation will appear: the muscles should bring the air to a complete standstill (see Ill. 27).

(d) Now let the air flow out of your mouth so gently and softly that you can only feel a little warmth against your hand. If you use the mirror again, you should see only a very thin film of condensation. As an extra exercise you can try, in one breath, to write your name in condensation on the glass of a window: this is very good for developing stamina in the respiratory muscles.

continues opposite

(e) Finally, close your mouth as in a kiss, and without adding more air pressure you will feel that increasingly a real airstream comes out. Be sure to keep the muscles involved in a tensed position (see Ill. 28).

Ill. 27

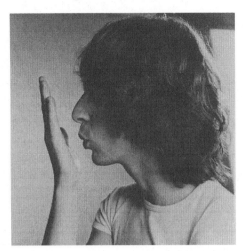

Ill. 28

What I have just described is, in principle, how the sound is produced on the recorder. The *windway* does what your lips were doing in Exercise 33(e): the *narrowing* of the windway speeds up the air until it becomes a real wind, just like a river that flows faster when it gets narrower. The little stream of air is almost all you need, while the tongue is responsible for separated notes. This means that with the help of a highly tensed air-pressure, the quantity of air used can be reduced to almost nothing.

Exercise 34

Repeat Exercise 33 and, while feeling the airstream, articulate some rhythmical "te-te-te-te" and "de-de-de-de". Notice the small "explosions" your tongue causes against your hand.

TAKE CARE:
Move only the tongue, not the cheeks or jaws

Finally the effect of this principle on playing. Earlier I explained that when breathing out you first use the air supported by the front, and secondly the air of the side breathing. Now the next idea should be a great help in learning to be very economical with your breath. It is based on the assumption that you keep you respiratory muscles expanded all the time during exhalation. If you get to the point that you cannot keep it up, it is again the front muscles that must sag first, then the side ones. This technique requires strong and well-trained muscles. So, please do not expect results too soon; well thought-out and systematic training and especially patience will be necessary. Laziness brings its own punishment.

50

When you have practised all these exercises very rigorously, and your respiratory muscles are strong, hard and supple, not weak or soft, only then will you realise that a complete inhalation is almost never necessary. The length of the musical sentence will provide the amount of air that you have to take in, no less, no more. When you sing, or even more when you talk, you will not easily take too much or too little air, because you are already so used to taking in automatically the right amount of air required for a particular phrase or sentence. The same applies to a musical sentence. However, it is a good idea to develop over-capacity to begin with.

Exercise 35

Repeat Exercise 32 and do it on a low F sharp

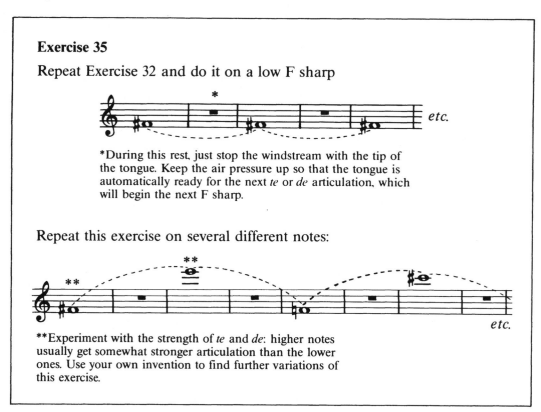

*During this rest, just stop the windstream with the tip of the tongue. Keep the air pressure up so that the tongue is automatically ready for the next *te* or *de* articulation, which will begin the next F sharp.

Repeat this exercise on several different notes:

**Experiment with the strength of *te* and *de*: higher notes usually get somewhat stronger articulation than the lower ones. Use your own invention to find further variations of this exercise.

The Tempo of the Inhalation

The up-beat (♪) that is reserved for the inhalation must be in complete agreement with the tempo and mood of the piece one is playing. A few examples:

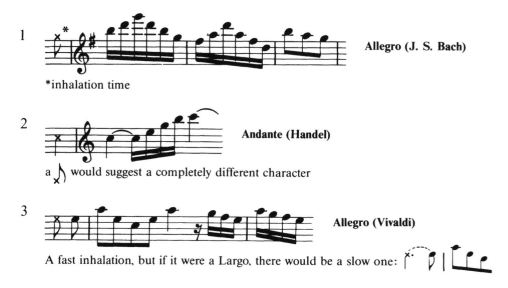

Allegro (J. S. Bach)

*inhalation time

Andante (Handel)

a ♪ would suggest a completely different character

Allegro (Vivaldi)

A fast inhalation, but if it were a Largo, there would be a slow one:

The fast inhalation

Often it is necessary to breathe very quickly in the middle of a passage, e.g.

In my remarks on Exercise 34 about the economical use of air, I emphasised the necessity to keep the respiratory muscles constantly expanded. If, when you have to take in another breath, both front and side muscles are relaxed, you have to expand the whole bunch of muscles again, which naturally takes rather a long time. If, however, all the muscles are still expanded, you have created a kind of vacuum, that can be filled up in a split second, if necessary.

Exercise 36

● Inhale as described

● Breathe in and out in the following rhythms, making sure that the respiratory muscles stay expanded all the time:

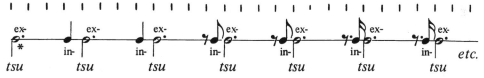

*Start each exhalation exactly on the beat with an audible "tsu", to make sure that you don't take more time for the inhalation than is given.

Use the metronome, and again:

● Keep all the respiratory muscles expanded all the time

● Interrupt the exhalation only with the tip of the tongue, not in the throat.

Some Remarks about the Mouth Cavity

For some reason certain recorder players try to influence the tone quality by making the mouth cavity bigger or smaller. Indeed, a large mouth cavity, with the lower jaw held low, does give a different sound from when the jaw is held up. But the difference is due not directly to the size of the mouth cavity, but to the speed of the airstream. It is a mistake to assume that a large and open mouth will provide nice resonance. You all know that the sound of the recorder is produced only where the air is divided, and that there is no way of improving the sound by making use of the space in the mouth.

A faster airstream gives a "faster" and a "thinner" sound, a slow one a "slower" and "fatter" tone; of course, it would be stupid not to make use of these possibilities. But the same effects can be produced more easily by changing the position of the tongue, by particular kinds of articulation, and by greater or lesser relaxation of the lips (see the next section). Holding the lower jaw very low is not a problem for the tone, but for the articulation: the tongue is pulled too far away from the palate, so that the tip has difficulty in making all the necessary kinds of movements. Because I don't want to anticipate later subjects (in this case vibrato), I will give you a standard mouth position, which keeps the way free for later modifications.

For secure control of the tone I have reasoned that the best place to prepare the sound is the one that is as close as possible to the windway. Keep both your lips, but especially the upper lip, relaxed, in such a way that the air can stream behind it, in fact between it and the teeth. In the following part you will learn to blow the air over the tip of the tongue, through the teeth against the back of the relaxed upper lip, the place where the tone will be "cooked" (vibrato, etc.) and from where it automatically will stream into the windway of the instrument.

An Exercise to Relax the Upper Lip

Exercise 37

An exercise to relax the upper lip:

- Place the recorder between the lips in a totally relaxed position (Ill. 29).

- Push the head-joint slowly upwards, so that the upper lip comes away from the teeth (Ill. 30).

- Push the recorder further upwards so that the upper lip will bounce back to the lower lip (Ill. 31).

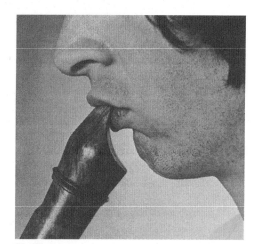

Ill. 29

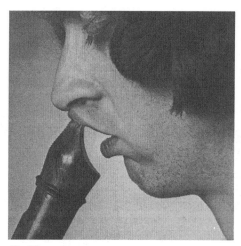

Ill. 30

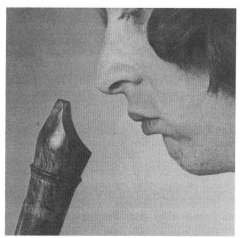

Ill. 31

I hope that I have made a rather complex subject clear enough to get you started. Please read carefully, and make sure that you understand the necessity of rigorous training. Have patience, for it can take some time before you notice any progress. It is not fair to ask your body to run 100 meters in under 10 seconds without any training! Start your training, and see how far you get.

Part IV

About Articulation

Just as all languages have their own rules about pronunciation, all musical instrumentalists have theirs: the violinist's right hand, the pianist's touch, the wind player's tonguing. The recorder — this so limited and restricted instrument — needs the tongue, the articulation more than all other wind instruments to pronounce its language. Playing the recorder without the tongue or with poor articulation is as unconvincing as a narrator with the same handicap: nobody will understand his story.

The particular tonguing problems that a player will have depend very much on the nature of his native language. Before a child is really conscious of his tongue, he already speaks his language fluently, and finds it difficult to adapt to the sounds of a different language. I have found that people who never have had the opportunity to study a foreign language often have difficulties in realising the problems involved with tonguing: English-speaking people often have problems with the *T*, the Japanese with *R*, and the French with any "double" articulation.

I mentioned in the preface that, mainly because of the demands of the avant-garde composers, it has become more and more inevitable that the recorder should develop its own specific articulation. The recorder is an extremely clear and direct instrument, and any articulation, however subtle, will have a perceptible effect; still is not such a long time ago that this part of recorder playing was regarded as being relatively unimportant. The forms of articulation that were used at first were taken directly from the most apparently similar orchestral instruments, especially the flute: slurs, single tonguing (*T-T-T* and *D-D-D*) and double tonguing (*T-K* and *D-G*).

I will try to explain a proper way to develop your articulation on the recorder, irrespective of your native tongue.

1 The Consonants
2 The Position of the Tongue with Single *T* and *D*
3 Double Tonguing with *T* and *D*
4 Double Tonguing with More than Two Syllables
5 Legato-Portato-Staccato
6 The Consonants *K* and *G*

1

The Consonants
Again the principle of naturalness applies here: we have to find the most normal and comfortable tongue movement that we can. For this reason I prefer to use as often as possible words of the language one is speaking. I am not giving you compulsory kinds of articulation; I am just presenting you with possibilities from which you can select.

One problem about this subject is that we are discussing things that happen inside the mouth, which are not visible from the outside, so the pictures that we have used up to now cannot help us this time.

In Exercise 34 we noticed little "explosions" against our hands with *te-te-te* and softer ones with *de-de-de*. It is essential to practise and understand these exercises very well before taking the next step: varying this *Te* and *De*.

We can distinguish between: *single* tonguing and
double tonguing.

The basic consonants

$$\left.\begin{matrix} T \\ D \\ R \end{matrix}\right\} : \text{ singles}$$

or any combination of them ——————— : doubles

and a combination of
one of these singles and the
'throat' syllables:

$$\left.\begin{matrix} K \\ G \end{matrix}\right\} : \text{ doubles}$$

In general *T* and *K* stand for a strong, *D* for a mild and *R* and *G* (as in "good" for a soft attack.*

* Later you will see that this can be reversible, so that T can be soft as well, *D* strong, etc., in various gradations.

2

The Position of the Tongue with Single T and D

For a long time it was thought that articulation could be greatly helped by a relaxed tongue free from any convulsive movements; the lower jaw was pulled down to create a large mouth cavity (supposedly to make the sound nice and round and mellow, with "resonance"), and to give space for the tongue. It was forgotten that the more the lower jaw is pulled down, the further the tip of the tongue has to travel to reach the palate, which means more effort than is strictly necessary; apart from that, it is not a very natural position for the jaw and tongue.

To take an analogy: If you want to move one finger very fast, you don't move the whole arm and hand, but you only move the finger (as in scratching your head).

The same works for the tongue: you should fix its position as much as possible (of course you mustn't force it down) so that only the tip is free to move, which it should do in a relaxed and easy way. To function properly, the tip needs the stability of the main body of the tongue.

The next exercise will give you a more comfortable tongue position.

Exercise 38

(a) Bring your back teeth together (gently, so that they are just touching — don't bite)

(b) Say "Cheddar". During the first half of this word you will feel the sides of your tongue touching (without pressing) the sides of your back upper teeth (please read this sentence several times!)

(c) Hold your tongue for a while in this "Che" position, and breathe normally. Be sure that you don't bite or get tense in any way.

(d) Now, by moving only the very tip of the tongue, say *da(r)-da(r)-da(r)-da(r)*, so, put together we get *Cheeeeeeeeedadadadadada(r)*. Be sure that you move only the tip, and keep the rest of the tongue where it is. If you combine this with Exercise 34 of the section on breathing, you will feel these little explosions against your hand again.

TAKE CARE:

Be sure you keep the teeth closed during this exercise and don't move your lower jaw as you might in normal speaking; later you can release the "bite" to a normal, that is almost closed position.

Problems that may arise:

☐ Moving, "chewing" lower jaw (a very common fault) — in this case close the teeth and "bite" a bit more.

☐ No "explosions": check the air pressure,

> make sure the throat is open (pushing down the larynx will result in closing of the trachea)

> keep everything as natural as possible, and if it helps, turn your head from left to right (always make sure that shoulders, legs and toes are not tense).

☐ No understanding of Ex. 38b: find your own word ("cheap"? "Yeah"?) and note again that no two mouths or tongues are shaped the same way.

☐ It is possible that the larynx is moving because the vocal chords are being used: in that case stop pronouncing the vowel sound (*eeee*), leaving only the consonant, so that no voiced sound is heard.

3

Double Tonguing with T and D

The Shape of the "Body" of the Tongue:

When I, for myself, compare the different movements that the tip of the tongue makes in pronouncing the words "teach" and "task", I notice that with "teach" the tip has a tendency to touch the palate a little further back, with the flattened tongue pressed against the back teeth, while with "task" the *a* brings the "body" of the tongue downwards and the tip slightly more forwards.

When actually pronouncing these words normally you will of course move the lips and jaw to some extent, but even with the more artificial pronunciation that we use when playing, (with the tongue and jaw fixed and without any vibration of the vocal chords) the tip of the tongue will still touch two different spots on the palate.

Exercise 39
- fix the tongue as in "Cheddar" or "Cheap"
- pronounce, first with the vocal chords, then without:

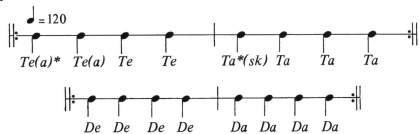

Te(a)* Te(a) Te Te   Ta*(sk) Ta Ta Ta

De De De De   Da Da Da Da

* as in "teach" and "task":

then play on the recorder:

Te Te De De   Ta Ta Da Da   Te te Da da   De de Ta ta   etc.

** Be sure you give a good air pressure

You will notice that with both *Ta* and *Da* the tone has the tendency to be a little lower in pitch: because of the wider mouth-cavity the air will move more slowly and the pitch will drop.

This is of course a very important conclusion and shows very clearly how essential it is to keep constant control over the position of the entire tongue, not just the very tip. It is a good idea to keep the tongue generally fixed in the *ea* position; it helps to make the articulation movement more natural. When you pronounce the verb "to DO" but suggest a diminuendo: *Todo* with *TO* on the beat — not *toDo*, you will realise that the tip of the tongue makes two different movements, one for the *T* and a slightly different one for the *D*. Now for the articulation on the recorder it is essential that with both these consonants — in spite of the two different movements that the tongue has to make to distinguish between the two sounds — the tip touches the same spot on the palate.

Once more, because no two mouths, tongues or palates are shaped the same, it is impossible to instruct you about the exact spot on the palate that the tongue touches for both sounds; however, with the help of the above exercises you should be able to find the most comfortable position for yourself. Let the tip of the tongue move to where it wants to, and don't force it into an unnatural position. As soon as you feel comfortable doing this exercise, repeat it as often as necessary until you have learned to recognise and remember the position of the spot on the palate.

It is very unlikely that the tip of the tongue will touch the back of the upper front teeth (I have never encountered this with any student). And of course it is absolutely wrong to touch the windway, because this will pull the tongue too much forward.

Even if the tip of the tongue touches the same spot on the palate with both *T* and *D*, you might have the idea that they feel different: the reason is that with *D* one uses a slightly smaller area of the tongue than with *T*; let's say that if *T* needs 2mm², *D* uses maybe only 1mm².

Again, in order to have a better tongue–"body" position, substitute *o* for *ea* during the next exercise.

Now while pronouncing *TeDeee* (for the time being you can use your voice again), feel the position of the tip of the tongue during the drawn out *Deeee*; you will notice that the tip "hangs around" somewhere in the mouth cavity: exactly where it stays or "hangs" is not important, but the essential thing is that the tip does not relax, but is prepared for the appearance of the next *T*.

We can say that, as long as the tip does not touch the palate, there will be sound: only the tip can interrupt the airstream that makes the sound. Some people stop the airstream with the throat or just stop blowing after each articulated note. I would strongly advise against this: it can make the musical line sound bumpy, and it will make it very difficult to achieve any regularity of articulation.

Exercise 40

(a) Sing at a comfortable pitch:

TeeeeDeeeeTeeeeDeeeeTeeeeDeeeeTe

(b) shorten this long *eee* gradually, not by stopping the exhalation but by interrupting the sound only with the tip of the tongue — the pressure stays constant.

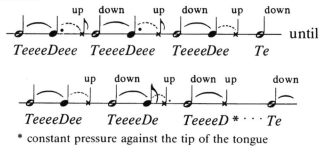

TeeeeDeee   TeeeeDee   TeeeeDee   Te

*TeeeeDee   TeeeeDe   TeeeeD * · · · Te*

* constant pressure against the tip of the tongue

So, after the tip of the tongue has pronounced the *D*, it jumps back up, to await the next instruction. In this exercise it's a *T*, but it can be any other consonant; it depends on how you like to start the new note.

With the help of the metronome ($\flat$ = 208), learn to use both consonants in strict time:

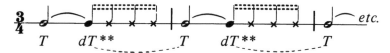

T   dT**   T   dT**   T

** *dT* is pronounced so quickly that it feels like one movement. and, while shortening the *Teee*, speed up until

T dT T dT T dT T dT T dT T dT T

TAKE CARE:

- *Be sure you don't relax the respiratory muscles and that the air pressure stays constant*
- *Keep the tongue in its fixed "Cheddar" position all the time*
- *Keep the teeth closed for the exercise. If you feel more comfortable with a more relaxed jaw, try lowering it a little, but remember that the faster the tongue has to move, the better a fixed tongue can support the tip. A "bite" only helps to fix the rest of the tongue better.*
- *Keep both lips free*
- *Be sure that only the tip of the tongue is responsible for the interruption of the sound.*
- *Don't allow your head, or (even more important) parts of the body to move together with the tongue.*

4

Double Tonguing with More than Two Syllables

Varying T and D

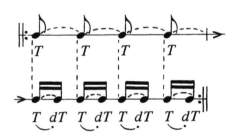

As you can see, in this example of double tonguing the first note of each pair is the longer, the second the shorter, the more staccato note. Before we talk about the different lengths notes can get (Section 5), let's first try to make both the same length.

In Exercise 40b the long-drawn *Teeeee* was followed by the shorter *Dee*. Now it will not take much imagination to think of them as a diminuendo, and it should not be too difficult to suggest the *d* as a result of the *T*: *Teeeedee*

The *T* causes the *d*, and together they are strictly contracted into one single action, with two results. So no extra air or energy has to be invested in the softer *d*. This means that the tongue is more or less responsible for the connection *T-d*, but not really for the reverse process *d-T*; it will not do this as easily and automatically as in the *T-d* connection. So the player carries the responsibility for the *d-T*. If he doesn't do anything, there will be a nice and smooth *T-d*, but from *d* back to *T* there will be automatically a little gap or obstruction (see the example below).

While in the previous exercises it was essential that the *d*-articulated note was as short as possible, in the following exercises we will make this note as long as possible, maybe even thinking of it as a crescendo in contrast to the diminuendo from *T* to *d*.

Exercise 41

(a)

becomes

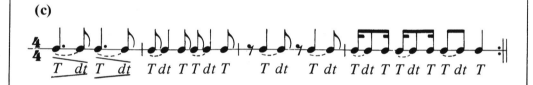

(b)

(c)

To begin with a slow tempo is recommended; later on you can speed up,

(d)

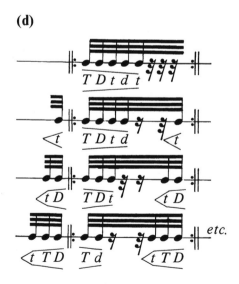

and make use of scales and all kinds of intervals:

continues opposite

*means a very legato-like articulation effect, which sounds almost similar to a really slurred interval. See the next section for more about this.

Playing Three Together: Adding the R

There is a third and even softer consonant which is necessary if one wants to articulate smoothly three notes together.

For people brought up with certain languages, such as Dutch, Italian and Swedish, it is not hard to understand the *R* produced by the tip of the tongue. For French, Japanese and certainly for English-speaking people this sound has very little to do with the *R* used in their native tongue (except maybe for Scottish people). I will try to explain this particular motion without talking really about this *R*. As I said, in some languages it is natural to pronounce the *R* with a very fast movement of the tip of the tongue, which is produced quite comfortably next to a *T* or *D*. However, this articulation will give an even more legato effect than that the *D* is able to provide.

Exercise 42

(a) Put the tongue in the "Cheap Cheddar" position

(b) Pronounce *Doodle*, but with a long drawn-out *oooo*, and give it a strong diminuendo as well: *Dooodle*.

(c) For the reasons explained above, replace the *ooooo* with *eeeeee*.

(d) Now, pronounce the whole word, except the very last part, the *le*, or, stop the sides of the tongue from leaking: *Deeeedl* — the tongue will "freeze" at the very last moment (between *d* and *l* one will hear a very short vowel: *Deeeeed(a)l*).

(e) It does not take much imagination to realise that the second *d* is a slightly different, rather milder tongue movement than the first *D* (compare "Denmark", "Sweden", "Daddy"). This second *d*, used as a single tonguing, can give a characterless and vague attack; however, used in combination with *T* and *D*, it will give a similar ease to the *T-D* combination given earlier, and after some practice it can even become more comfortable.

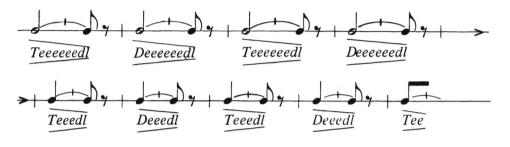

TAKE CARE:

Be sure that this soft d *does not become a sort of fat* l *with hardly any articulation effect: it must be, of course, a usable articulation, as effective as the others are.*

(f) After practising the *Deedle* combination thoroughly, it will not be hard to substitute *T* for *D*

Teeeeeedl   *Deeeeeedl*   *Teeeeeedl*   *Deeeeeedl*

Teeedl   *Deeedl*   *Teeedl*   *Deeedl*   *Tee*

To avoid confusion, I will call this *dl* articulation *R/r*.

In Exercise 41(a) we lengthened the *T-d* combinations, now we can do the same with the *T-R* and *D-R* combinations.

Exercise 43

Repeat Exercise 41 and replace *dt* with *rt* and alternate them.

Earlier I talked about one action, one articulation with two effective results

$$T - d, \quad D - r, \quad T - r$$

Now we also can involve the *R* in it and make combinations with three effective results, like:

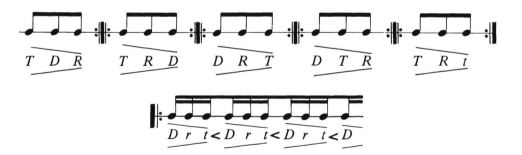

T D R   *T R D*   *D R T*   *D T R*   *T R t*

D r t < D r t < D r t < D

It is a good idea to find connecting words in your native language, which will almost automatically provide convenient combinations of consonants suitable for articulation on the recorder, like, for example, *T D R* in English, where the combination *Todo (Tede)* and the *Doodle (Deedle)* can give the artificial word *TeDedle (TeDeRe)*, or where "Dative" will give you the difference between *D* and *t*, etc.

Now we can even go one step further by varying the separate singles *T, D* and *R*. For example, when we take a single articulation using only *T*s, all the notes sound completely equal, but instead you can pronounce every second *T* a little softer, as at the end of a diminuendo, so that instead of

 you pronounce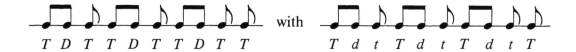

(compare *tiTAnic* and *TEtanus*).

This small *t* is really a *T* movement of the tongue (and absolutely not a kind of *D* or *R*), only it is not pronounced as a new start (*T*), but more as the result of the first *T*.

Compare

 with

T D T T D T is a succession of single syllables, which provides a nice and useful effect, but which definitely limits the speed at which it can be done.
T d t T d t uses a single (*tT*) as well, but, because the *t* has a slightly different position, it makes the connection with big brother *T* easier, and results in a smoother effect.

The next exercise uses several combinations of *T, D* and *R*.

Exercise 44

resulting accentuation

With what you learned in Exercise 41(d), you can make the accents I gave above more or less clear, purely by means of the articulation and without any support from the breath.

Playing Four and More Syllables Together

It is also possible to combine four different syllables, as it were four by four.

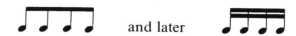

and later

can be articulated as follows:

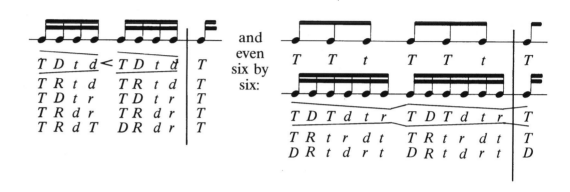

and even six by six:

Eight by eight is not really possible, and is generally done four by four, with the start of the second four softer:

Here it is important to take note of Exercise 41(d) and the connection between the softest *r* and the next new start *T* or *t*. A little explanation may help here: when you articulate as described above, that is more or less a four by four articulation, you make a different grouping in musical terms, for instance five and three, in such a way that the diminuendo overlaps the first five notes and the other three are used for the up-beat crescendo again.

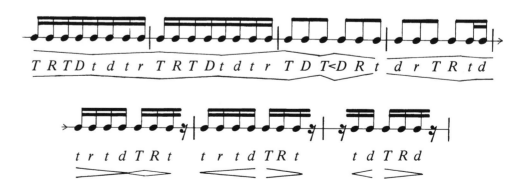

After thorough practice, all the consonants used (*T, D, R, t, d, r*) should give an equally clear articulation, so much so that the outsider, the listener, hears a series of similar tonguings, which he can experience as singles. And that is not as simple as it sounds: the *D(d)* and certainly the *R(r)* are softer tonguings than the *T(t)*, with less explosive effect, which means that they automatically will sound softer, or even further away. You should learn to give them a little accent, by doing some exercises with the *T* on the upbeat:

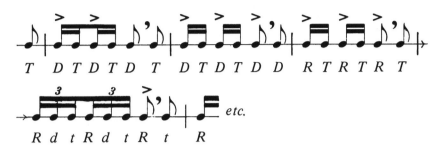

You should really aim for a succession of notes that sound completely equal; only you the player, knows what kind of articulation you use — we, the listeners, only hear an easy, natural sequence of clearly articulated notes. It's obvious that you should do these exercises on the recorder on all fingerings, not forgetting the lowest and highest notes of the instruments

NOTE
During all these exercises the movement of the tongue is in principle always two by two or three by three: *TD, DR, TR, TDt, Tdr, DrT*, etc.

Problems to be expected:
These can be innumerable! To solve some of the more important ones try the following:

☐ Check the position of the tongue; close the teeth if necessary

☐ Make sure the tip of the tongue always touches the same spot on the palate

☐ Don't push the lower jaw back, forwards or down

☐ Be sure your Adam's apple does not move

☐ Don't tighten the throat

☐ Check that you can feel the sides of the tongue against the back teeth all the time

☐ Keep the air pressure constant

☐ Be sure all the consonants used sound clear.

It is most important that it should all feel as natural as possible. Analyse all these hints above and use the ones that appeal to you.

5

Legato-Portato-Staccato

The length of a particular note is controlled by the kind of articulation the next note gets.

Exercise 45

(a) play a long g″

(remember the exercises done for breathing)

(b) The *T*, compared with *D* or *R*, is by itself a rather sharp tonguing, with a strong presence; it uses a relatively large part of the tip of the tongue, and therefore takes more time than *D* or *R*. That results automatically in a small gap between each *T*-articulated note.

(c) put your tongue in the familiar "Cheddar" position and articulate

g″:

Teeeeeee Teeeeeee Teeeeeee Teeeeeee Teeeeeee Teee

all exactly of the same length and quality.
Be sure that only the tip of the tongue interrupts the sound!

(d) the *D*-articulation uses less tongue "body" and therefore results in

g″:

D eeeeeeeDeeeeeeeDeeeeeeeDeeeeeeeDeeeeeeeDeee

an almost portato result, while

(e) *R* will give an legatissimo effect that is only just articulated:

g″:

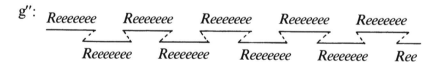

Reeeeeee Reeeeeee Reeeeeee Reeeeeee Reeeeeee
Reeeeeee Reeeeeee Reeeeeee Reeeeeee Ree

One note, as it were, interrupts the previous one, or the tones overlap each other.

Paradoxically, this last articulation is used very frequently in slow pieces, in spite of the fact that it has to be the fastest one.
With *TeeTeeTee* and to a lesser extent *DeeDeeDee* the tongue has more time to make its movement than with *ReeReeRee*.

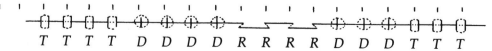

T   T   T   T   D   D   D   D   R   R   R   R   D   D   D   T   T   T

Exercise 46

This is an example of how to study the next fragment (Handel's Sonata in C)

- Check the air pressure is constant
- Don't blow too hard or too soft, just normally
- Practise each example with the following articulations (and others):

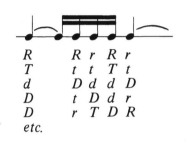

R	R	r	R	r
T	t	t	T	t
d	D	d	d	D
D	t	D	d	r
D	r	T	D	R
etc.				

How to End a Note

Talking about how to begin a note automatically means that I have to explain to you how to end a note.

The length of a note is determined only by the tongue, and, in general, never by stopping the supply of air (slackening the air pressure will definitely spoil the tone quality). You have to realise that the movement of the tip can be divided into an upward and a downward one, even in the very fast *R*-tonguing. With the previous exercise

Reeeeeee   Reeeeeee

Reeeeeee   Reeeeeee

you only have to think about the downward movement: that one results in an audible articulation, and automatically implies that there should be an upward one as well. The next example shows you that you can increasingly separate these two movements.

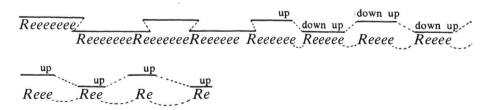

Each beginning, each down movement, is exactly on time with the metronome, but endings, the upward movements, will be done gradually earlier and earlier, and will make the audible sound shorter (the constant air pressure of course will not be affected). In rhythmic terms the upward movement should have an upbeat character; this is important for keeping the connection between the up and down movements: both parts of the whole movement are still just as much connected.

Reeeeeeee _____ up   Reeeeee   down up   Reeeee

T   Reeeeeeeee   down up   Reeeee   down

D

*note the rhythmic connection between up and down.

Generally speaking I can recommend that you should end the last note of each phrase or sentence by cutting off the airstream with the tip of the tongue. This cutting off is nothing more than the up-and-down movement of the the tip of the tongue described above. During this action be sure the speed of the upward movement of the tongue is without force, but not too slow: it should in general be as late as possible and related to the tempo and character of the piece.

R will give a very soft ending, but with the danger that the air pressure may drop at the very end of the note, so that it goes out of tune. If this happens, the pitch can be corrected by a very small and short "shot" of air at the end of the note, which is not audible, but only intended to keep the note in tune. However, this is not easy, and is only worth the trouble in special cases.

T, on the other hand, will tend to give a rather abrupt ending, this time with the danger that the pitch will rise at the very end of the note, though again it is possible to correct this with the air pressure.

It's more comfortable to use the *D*-ending, which is suitable for almost any context.

It really depends on the character of the piece which consonant is best for the ending. However, just as it is essential to take the beginning of a note seriously, the ending of the note must be made with discretion.

Another method is to stop the sound only by cutting off the airstream, while the tip of the tongue stays down. I cannot see the point of this myself, especially considering that with this method it is hard to stop the pitch dropping at the end of the note, unless one injects an unnaturally strong gust of air at the end. Only when one has to breathe very fast can one really use this technique.

Staccato   Please realize that it's not the beginning of the tone that guarantees you the characteristic short sound of staccato, but more the very moment the tongue- tip (or larynx with *K* and *G*) ends the sound by stopping the airstream. Staccato actually is nothing more than a shortened portato. With portato, or 'legatissimo' the tip touches the palate for as short a time as possible, while with staccato the tongue stays up for as long as possible. The upward movement can be seen as just one half of the total action, but is as a move related to one of the downward movements *T, D, R* or *K* and *G*. It is comparable with the moves the tongue-tip makes going from the first to the second *t* in *Stitch* (see Exercise 32): *stitch*.

articulations: *Td, Tt, Dr*, etc.

Be sure that you keep up a constant air pressure; don't 'blow' for each note!

Once more: staccato can be articulated with the singles *T, D, R, K* or *G*, depending on the function and character that you want to give the notes, and also with any combination of these consonants.

For a smooth and elegant staccato, one should use the combinations of consonants as with the more portato and legato combinations. A single articulation is possible, of course, but it will limit the speed and comfort.

Problems to be expected

☐ An irregular staccato line because of

- inhalation between each note
- insecure pronunciation
- "chewing" lower jaw (keep the teeth closed for the moment)

☐ Irregular gusts of volume

- check that the air pressure is constant,
- keep thinking in long melody lines
- vary the combination of consonants.

Going gradually from legato, via portato to "super-staccato", the nuances are very subtle. In contrast to the idea that you have to learn to *hear* these differences, I can strongly recommend that you concentrate more on how these articulations *feel*.

Learn to remember the specific feeling belonging to a particular articulation. Don't play *TDR* only by listening, but also, and perhaps to a greater extent, learn to recognize the physical feeling. Don't get this wrong: the fact that these nuances are not always easy to distinguish may give you the notion that don't have to be taken seriously; however, after mastering all these subtleties, you will have the ability to pronounce your own person musical "story" as you want to, — isn't it this what you are studing for?

The next exercise will help you in this.

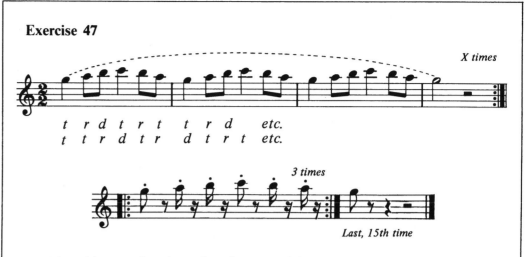

- Play this exercise slurred at first, so without using the tongue, and as one melody line.
- Then, for the second time, play the line legatissimo, so with very smooth tonguing.
- Then play it about fifteen times, each time with fractionally shorter notes, so that you end up with a "super-staccato".

If done well, the gradual development will be so subtle, that the outsider cannot actually hear the differences — the listener always hears the differences later.

It is obvious that the same exercise should be done in reverse as well, starting with the staccato and ending with slurring.

Of course, after using the given articulations, you should find your own combinations, and practise them seriously.

6

The Consonants K and G

The so-called "double staccato" *T-K* and its milder equivalent *d-g*, should, generally speaking, only be used in fast passages.

Although it is possible to create fine nuances with these articulations in any tempo, we have found that in slower tempi the *T, D* and *R* can provide more variety.

The term "double staccato" (taken from the terminology of flute playing) comes from the effect you get almost automatically with *T-K*; although it is possible to get a smoother sound with *T-K*, *d-g* (*g* as in "giggle") easily gives a lighter effect.

The main problem here is that the "explosions" created by *K* or *g* are so much further away from the instrument than those made by *T, D,* or *R*, that they can easily sound softer, and more distant, especially if the respiratory muscles are not providing a constant breath pressure. If the air has to get its speed from these distant "explosions", they must be so strong, that it becomes difficult to create nuances. With a constant pressure the air already has its own speed, and the articulations only "colour" the sound.

To solve this problem, do the next exercise in which you substitute *K-T* for *T-K* and and *g-d* for *d-g*.

Fast

T	K	T	K	T	K	T	K	T	K		T		K	T	K	T	K	T	K
d	g	d	g	d	g	d	g	d	g		d		g	d	g	d	g	d	g
T	k	d	g	T	k	d	g	T	k		d		g	T	k	d	g	T	k	d	g
t	g	d	K	t	d	g	K	t	g		d		K	t	g	d	K	t	g	d	K

☐ staccato and legatissimo

☐ aim for total evenness: — *K* should sound like *d* and *g*.

As with the tip of the tongue the throat movement can be divided into an upward and a downward one, which means here that the tone produced by the downward movement of the tongue is stopped by the upward movement of the throat, and the reverse (see the story about how to end a note).

I have found that some people like the idea of playing the *T* and *K* as far away from each other as possible, while others on the contrary like to bring them as close to each other as possible, as if in the words *Dinkey* or *Bingo*, becoming *Tinkey* and *Dingo*.

Experiment until you have found your own personal pronunciation. The following exercise will help you develop this.

Exercise 48

Take the fingering *1234567* and blow so gently that you do not hear the g″ that should come from this particular fingering, but a very soft and thin sort of b′ flat. If it is hard enough already to keep this note straight (you need a high air pressure), you will find it really difficult to pronounce a very smooth "legatissimo" *d-g* or *T-K*. Notice how much slower the throat moves naturally than the tip of the tongue does, and how easily the tone jumps to a higher f′ or g″.

pppp

T	k	T	k		T	k	T	k		T		k		T	k	T	k	T		k		k		T
D	g	T	k		d	g	t	k		D		G		k	d	g	T	k	D		g		g
k	k	k	k		G	G	g	g		T		t		g	g	g	g	k	'R'		g		d

etc.

Another suggestion: give the *K* or *g* little accents, make them stronger, giving them more attention:

   until all notes sound equal.

T K d g T K d g T:

As with the *T-D-R* combinations, put 2, 3, 4 or more notes together in a physical diminuendo/crescendo in order to relax (see also the next volume, the part about scales). Don't play these exercises too slowly.

More specialised kinds of articulation will be found in the following volumes.

Exercise 49